Dream Rooms

SMART TALK

Dream Rooms
Decorating with Flair

Victoria Sherrow

Troll Associates

Library of Congress Cataloging-in-Publication Data

Sherrow, Victoria.
   Dream rooms, decorating with flair / by Victoria Sherrow;
illustrated by Diana Magnuson.
      p.   cm.—(Smart talk)
   Summary: Presents tips for girls on how to create the room of
their dreams.
   ISBN 0-8167-2293-5 (lib. bdg.)   ISBN 0-8167-2294-3 (pbk.)
   1. Interior decoration—Juvenile literature. [1. Bedrooms.
2. Interior decoration.]   I. Magnuson, Diana, ill.   II. Title.
III. Series.
NK2115.S48   1991
747.7′7—dc20   90-48241

Table of Contents

Your Room Is Your Castle

*L*ife can get hectic. You rush from school to sports and other activities. There are chores to do at home and homework to finish. Then comes the weekend—more chores, maybe an afternoon at the movies, a sleep-over, a birthday party or an hour to finish that super mystery you've been reading.

You need a place to unwind and get a good night's sleep just to keep up with it all! You need a place to organize your clothes, school papers and sports

1

and hobby equipment, a place to keep your books and records, a place to be all by yourself. That special place is, of course, your room.

How can one room—or maybe just a part of a shared room—do all these important things for you? That's what this book is all about. You'll learn how to take a fresh look at the space you have. You'll see what your needs are—and whether a few changes could help meet them better. Then comes the *real* fun: dozens of ideas for jazzing up everything from walls and floors to your dresser and desk. Best of all, most of these ideas depend on your own effort and imagination. They use materials that you already have or can buy without spending lots of money.

IS IT TIME FOR A CHANGE?

No matter how great the room looks to an outsider, just about everybody dislikes *something* about her room. Maybe you can barely squeeze everything into a tight closet. Or maybe your drawers seem so small that even one of Snow White's dwarves couldn't fit his stuff inside. Sometimes it seems that there's no room for sports and hobby equipment . . . and no place to show off your trophies, glass animals, scrapbooks or other collections. Or even to study!

These space and organization problems can interfere with your daily life. You find yourself wasting time and energy looking for things and shaking wrinkles out of T-shirts that got squashed in a crowded drawer. Luckily, there are ways to solve these problems. You can change your room from

2

Change your room from "messy" to "marvelous" with a little creativity and little money.

3

"messy" to "marvelous"—and this book will show you how.

Maybe you don't like the way your room *looks* right now—the colors aren't really "you," the walls are blah or the style is too babyish. If your family has some extra cash, you can shop for a floor-to-ceiling redecoration. But few families can afford new furniture or designer curtains and wallpaper. Working with your parents and sticking to a budget are important parts of decorating your room. A tight budget might even be an *advantage*—you will probably end up designing a room that is much more special, with more of *your* personality, by using your head and hands as well as your wallet.

Decorating your room—and solving the problems that go with the job—is part of the whole business of growing up. It's the beginning of the lifelong fun of putting your own touch on the world around you. Just as you have a style in choosing clothes, you also have a decorating style. Maybe you don't know what it is yet. Finding out will be part of the fun!

So, what does *your* room need, and what does it need the most? Will you be changing something big, like the color, or just adding a few special touches? Do you and your sister have to choose new bedspreads to replace the worn-out ones? Are you finally going to clean out your closet (the *whole* closet), or can you move right on to making pen holders or pillow covers?

Read on and find out!

Getting Started

What do you do in your room? Well, you sleep there, of course. But chances are your room is also the place for several other activities such as dressing, reading, doing homework, writing letters, drawing or working on other hobbies like dancing, exercising or practicing a musical instrument. You may have over a dozen activities that all require their own space and storage.

Great rooms start with planning! If you take some time to think about the way your room could work for you, you can find ways to meet those needs better. The result will be a room that is not only nice to look at, but also works well for *you*.

TAKE A LOOK AROUND

Start by taking a good look at your room the way it is *now*. Get a notebook and pen and make a few notes. Below is a check list that you can use to organize yourself.

☆☆ **INSPECTION CHECK LIST** ☆☆

1. **Room Measurements/Furniture:** What size is your room? You can't change the room's measurements, but you can arrange the furniture and organize your things to make the most of the space you have. Measure the width and length of the room and jot down the figures in your notebook. Describe the furniture and where it is placed.

2. **Storage Space:** Check out your storage space. Do you have your own closet? Does the closet have other storage features—shelves, extra hanging bars, etc.? Do you have shelves—either on the wall or in a bookcase? How about dresser drawers? How many? Are they overcrowded? How about a dresser-top? You might actually have the storage space, but if you're like most of us, you will need to plan a good "cleanup session" before you know how much you have.

3. **Activity Areas:** A study area is usually a "must." It can be anything from a fancy wooden desk full

of drawers and pigeonholes to a table with some storage containers. What is your study/work area like? Do you already have one or will you need to make one? If you have one, how well does it work? Do you need a bulletin board, or some extra drawers, stacking units or containers for desk items? What else do you do in your room? Are there activities or equipment that have no place at all? Make a note of them.

4. **Bed and Other Furniture:** What is your bed like? Is it a twin size or larger? What do you think of your bedclothes—sheets, pillow covers, bedspread or quilt? Are they worn out? Would colorful new trimming improve their looks? Does your bed give you extra seating space when your friends come over to do homework or listen to music? What other seating space do you have? A desk chair or some floor pillows? Grandma's old rocker or a modern camp-style chair? Do you have the seating space that you need?

5. **Walls and Windows:** Look at the walls, floors, curtains (or other window treatments), doors and trim. How do you like the colors and prints? Does everything go well together? What needs the most help?

6. **Carpet or Other Flooring:** Do you have a carpet? Is it a nice color and pattern? Can you "lift" colors from it for the rest of the room? If you have a wood or tile floor, is it warm and cozy or could it use a throw rug?

7. **Things I Need:** Have you found that there are things missing that you really *need*? For example,

a warm comforter or a larger dresser. List these things here.

8. **Things I Want:** Are there some specific things that you feel would just make your room special? You don't really *need* them but . . . a big pillow, maybe, or some new curtains. These things go here.

9. **Things I Would Like:** These are things that you could see going in your room, eventually. These could be long-term projects like embroidering a cushion or building a headboard.

10. **Special Touches:** These are the little things that make your room unique. First, list the ones you have (your collections, that quilt your grandmother made for you, etc.), and then list the ones you would like.

11. **Overall Effect:** How do you feel about your room in general? Is it bright and cheery or a little drab? Do you love the color or hate it? What special touches might give it a lift or make it just more *you*?

☆☆☆

Finding out problems is the first step in solving them. Don't get discouraged—there are ways to deal with all the space and decorating problems above. And many solutions can be done on a tight budget!

THERE'S THIS ONE
SMALL PROBLEM . . .

Okay, you say. I'm willing to clean things up and reorganize. And I'm a "crafty" person; I'll take the time and effort to make my room look better, with the help of some good ideas. But! My sister shares the room with me, and:
1. She is a total slob.
2. She plays the trumpet in the school band (which means she usually wants to practice while I'm studying).
3. We don't even like the same colors.

How to share a room and get along with your roommate is a problem that has puzzled people since we lived in caves. But it *can* be done. It takes good communication, some bargaining and a few compromises.

WHEN IT'S NOT YOUR MESS

If you're not messy but you share a room with your sister and she is, the first and most important thing to do is talk about the problem with her: She might not even know it bothers you. If "Miss Messy" doesn't change, you can still clean up your own bed and section of the room and keep them looking great. Watching your good example might help her messy ways, but if it doesn't, don't keep harping on it—that'll only make her worse.

One of the first things to do when you share is to divide up the room fairly and clearly. The closet space can be split right in half, and so can the drawers, shelves and so on. Make a list of chores to rotate—like vacuuming or dusting. Or each girl can be in charge of cleaning her own defined space. The important thing is to make clear whose space, belongings and chores are whose.

DIVIDE AND CONQUER

Sharing a room doesn't mean that you have to be together every second. There are ways of dividing up a room so that you can have your own space and some privacy. If the room is big enough, you can place each twin bed lengthwise against opposite walls with a chest of drawers in between the heads of the beds. Each girl can have a trunk at the bottom of the bed—to be used as storage and an extra seat.

Dividing your room in half helps both you and your

Two tables or desks at opposite ends of the room will provide separate study areas. Put a bookshelf in between the study areas if there's enough room. Large objects—like bookcases or even a tall plant—can separate your part from hers.

If your room is small, use a "visual divider" on the wall to separate two different areas. Borders of wallpaper can be pasted down the middle and around the top of the wall to make a rectangle around each bed; stripes of paint can also divide the two areas. If you have a movable folding screen or can make or buy one, this is a good way to divide the space. You can also put hooks on such a screen and hang things on them—extra storage.

Try bargaining for space: Maybe you have more books and she has more clothes? In that case, you could trade some closet space for more than half the

roommate find some personal space.

11

bookshelf. Bargaining works for other things, too—
like dividing up chores.

COLOR CONTROVERSIES

What if you can't agree on colors? Maybe she likes
red and you like green, or you're hassling over teal
blue and fuchsia? There are lots of ways to compromise on the color issue. If you're choosing new
sheets, bedspreads, curtains or wallpaper, you can
pick a print that includes both your favorites. Or
compromise—she picks the wall color, you choose
the sheets.

Some girls solve the "color problem" by using
their own colors in their own spaces. This works
particularly well if your colors are compatible. Cindy
and Paula decided on white walls. There were two
closets so Paula had her door painted sky blue and
Cindy opted for peach. Each girl picked sheets in
her favorite color but the comforters are in blue and
peach floral design. Each girl decorated her study
table with containers and accessories in either blue
or peach—using clay pieces made at school, fabric,
ribbons and stick-on paper from a variety store.
They also bought paper in peach and sky blue to
make mats for the pictures over their beds. The
curtains are blue and white stripes with peach
ribbon ties.

Amy and Joan did something similar with a red,
white and blue color scheme. They even spray-
painted some bricks in red and blue, to hold up
white painted boards for shelves. Each girl covered
the frame of her desk blotter with red or blue
corduroy. It's easy to tell whose things are whose

with this kind of "color coding." (Some girls use stickers or stick-on initials for the same purpose.)

The problem gets harder when the colors you each like just don't mix. In that case, you might have to bargain. You get your choice this time; next time the room is repainted, she gets hers. Or you'll give in on color, but you get to pick the dresser or the style of curtains or carpet.

MAKING ROOM

What if your roommate is much younger than you are? You can talk to your parents about the problem and plan a room that suits both your needs. Pick wall and floor colors that are neutral enough for both ages.

For example, you could have a sun-gold carpet on the floor so that the young child can have pastel plaids on her bed, but you can pick brighter-colored stripes on yours. Each of you can add special touches to your own sides of the room, especially if the basic colors and furniture are versatile enough for you both.

And what about privacy? Some girls work out an arrangement that lets each of them have private time in the room. You and your roommate can agree on a period of "alone time" in the room on a regular basis. The time can be used for listening to music, practicing on an instrument or dance routine, spreading out a science project or just sitting quietly to think.

SHARING ISN'T ALL BAD

By now, you have some ideas about how to share with your roommate. You know that it's important to talk things out, bargain, get help from your parents and be clear about who has what and who does what.

It's also good to remember the *nice* things about sharing a room. If you and your roommate aren't too far apart in age, you have someone to talk to and share jokes with. You can listen to music together, help each other with stubborn zippers and French-braid each other's hair.

If you are several years older, remember that your younger sister probably looks up to you. She is eager to "be big" and learn the things that you know—how to draw, how to sew and how to roller-skate. Try to see her as more than just a "pest." And if your sister is several years older than you, just think of all the things you can learn from her! She can tell you all about social skills and talking to your parents, about clothes and makeup and even share the decorating ideas she's picked up. Just remember that she probably likes to be alone sometimes too, and try to give her the space she needs.

By sharing a room, you can learn valuable lessons about getting along with people—lessons that will help you in the years to come. You can also learn a lot by cooperating with your parents and siblings as you plan ways to fix up your room. Sharing has its problems, but loneliness isn't one of them. And later on, you may have many nice memories of those years that you spent sharing a room!

14

Bye-Bye Budget Blues

"*I* might as well forget about fixing up my room," says Lynn. "It's a mess, but we can't afford new furniture, carpets, curtains or anything." Maybe you find yourself in the same situation; many people do. Necessities tend to use up most or all of the family budget, leaving very little for decorating.

Never fear! Facing a "cash crunch" doesn't mean you can't do anything with your room. You can do a lot to brighten up your space with the few dollars you can earn baby-sitting or raking a neighbor's leaves, and we bet there's a lot of stuff around your home you could use if you thought about it.

Think about the best-dressed girls you know. Are they always the ones with the most money to spend on new clothes? Often, the most stylish girls are the ones who do interesting things with the clothes they have, who put their outfits together "just so." They find unusual accessories to give old clothes a lift and combine colors in fresh, clever ways. It's the same with decorating a room—money isn't everything!

Decorating on a tight budget may take more time and creativity, but it can also be more fun—and more personal. And won't you feel proud when you show off the results?

HIDDEN TREASURES

How can you fix up your room without much cash? One way is to find things that are free (or almost free). Take a nice long "tour" of Grandma's attic. Look in your own attic, too. Or, if you don't have an attic, try the storage room or closet. Hidden in the deep, dark recesses there are sure to be a few treasures, such as:

- ✪ *Pieces of fabric, old scarves, lace and ribbon trims, beads—anything that can be used for pillows, curtain trim, etc.*
- ✪ *Old picture frames that nobody wants—they can be cleaned up, even stripped of old paint or varnish and given a whole new look.*
- ✪ *Slightly damaged pieces of furniture. These can be fixed, repainted or stained if they are not in good*

16

shape. (You can do the same with the tired-looking furniture already in your room.)

✪ *Pillows with worn-out covers—these can be recovered in a variety of ways.*

✪ *Spare jars, dishes and bottles—decorate and use them as containers on your dresser, table or desk.*

✪ *An old rug that can be cleaned and used; pieces of carpet that can be made into an area rug.*

✪ *Clay pots and other containers to use for plants.*

✪ *Ship models, plaques for the wall or an old sculpture or painting that can make interesting decorations.*

You can never really predict what you might come up with or what you could use it for. When Maria and her family moved to a new house, Maria browsed through the attic and found a large seashell that the previous owners no longer wanted. Maria cleaned the seashell and put it on her desk—first it held her homemade potpourri; later it became a holder for calligraphy pens.

SHOPPING SAVVY

Shopping wisely is the key to buying things on a tight budget and there are some places that every bargain hunter should know about. Most towns have some *flea markets or secondhand stores*, or they are near enough to visit. Goodwill and Salvation Army stores often sell secondhand furniture, as well as other things you might need.

Discount stores or outlets sell everything from wallpaper and paint to hardware and closet organizers at low prices. There are even some outlet stores that

*Hidden treasures are easily found for next-to-nothing at
yard sales and flea markets.*

18

specialize in home-decorating supplies and furnishings.

You can buy wooden chairs, tables, desks, bookshelves, etc., at *unfinished furniture stores*. The items you get in these stores have to be painted or stained (with a wood finish). They are less expensive than already-finished furniture and it can be a lot of fun to finish them yourself.

You can also find inexpensive furniture, storage items, closet organizers, fabrics, sheets, curtains and area rugs in *variety stores, drugstores or five-and-dime stores*. These stores also have accessories—pillows and pillow forms, lace and other trims, containers and desk organizers.

Wendy bought a batch of pretty paisley scarves at a five-and-dime store and used them to cover pillows. Kate found just the stacking units she needed to clean up the mess on her desk. Barbara bought some inexpensive plain window shades and decorated them with designs cut from self-sticking paper. There are many more possibilities. (Watch for sales at these stores, too!)

Yard sales are the greatest for finding useful odds and ends. Check the newspaper for ads to see when people in town are planning a weekend yard sale, tag sale or garage sale. Also keep an eye on the ads if you are looking for a bed, mattress or other major accessory.

Do you need a desk? If you haven't had any luck with yard sales or secondhand stores, you could see if your town's *school system* sells its discarded desks. With a parent's help, you may be able to get one of these ex-school desks at a very reasonable price.

Often, the *yellow pages* of the phone book are

helpful. Your friends and their parents may also know where to shop for bargains, so start asking!

EVALUATING YOUR FINDS

When you're buying sale items or secondhand furniture, you need to check them carefully before you buy. A bargain is no bargain if it turns out to be unusable!

Here are some things you and your parents can think about:

✪ *Is the piece you are planning to buy well-made?*
✪ *Can it be painted if the old finish is ruined?*
✪ *Can it be repaired if some of the parts are loose, broken or missing?*
✪ *If the item is stained or dirty, can it be cleaned at home successfully?*
✪ *If it has holes, can they be mended? Or can an inexpensive cover be put on something like a worn-out chair seat?*

Even if you are not in a buying mood, browsing through stores and yard sales may give you some good ideas. It may also help you to plan ahead for the time when you can afford the item you want.

If you and your parents decide to fix up old furniture, there are many helpful books available. The manufacturers of refinishing and paint products offer instruction pamphlets. There are also books in the library that give directions for repairing and finishing furniture.

SEW IT GOES

Do you know how to sew or do you know someone who does? Sewing skills come in handy throughout life, so you may want to take a class at school or learn from a grownup. If you do know someone who sews (maybe your mother or grandmother), you might ask for help on things that your room needs—new curtains, pillow covers or a seat cushion for your chair. Maybe you could do a special favor or chore in exchange for the help.

Whether you sew or not, a fabric store can be a real help in fixing up your room. You'll find fabrics in all kinds of colors, prints and textures to spark your imagination. Fabric stores also have all kinds of other things for decorating your room: lace and other trims, kits for making accessories like pillows, and patterns for dresser scarves, pillows, table covers and curtains. Some have needlepoint kits, as well as kits for making hooked rugs and for covering cardboard hatboxes with pretty wallpaper. There are also special crayons and fabric paints for "do-it-yourself" designs on pillowcases, bedcovers and curtains. So, even if you can't sew, visit your local fabric store for ideas.

And don't forget to ask the clerk where you can find the "remnant bin." Almost every fabric or sewing store has a shelf or bin full of "remnants"— leftover pieces of fabric that are reduced in price from the regular cost per yard. These pieces may not be large enough for big projects, but they are good for things like pillow covers. Some stores even sell drapery and upholstery remnants. While you're at it, you can also snap up some pretty lace, trim, buttons, kits and ribbons in the remnant bin!

Carla found enough fabric remnants and trims to make a fluffy pile of pillows for her bed. Carla likes frilly things so she picked pastel colors and white fabrics, with lace trim to match. Some pieces of fabric weren't large enough for both sides of a square pillow, so Carla made pillows that have different colors on each side. They looked super!

By now, you've learned many tricks for getting things either free or at least at a more reasonable price. You'll learn about other budget-savers for windows, walls, beds, floors and work areas in the following chapters.

The main point to remember is this: You can outwit the cash crunch—great rooms *are* possible on a budget!

Making the Most of Your Space

O ne good way to save money when fixing up your room is to realize what you already have. Cleaning up and organizing your stuff can help you find out what you need, what you already have and how to show it off to its best. Remember, cleaning up and organizing doesn't cost a dime. If you've been putting it off, just remember the last time you lost your homework under a sweater or a stack of old magazines. Or maybe you were late for a great party because your favorite belt was buried in the tangled mess on your closet floor. You might even have missed a soccer match when you had forgotten to fix a broken shoestring—you had just kicked your cleated shoes under the bed and thought you'd remember them "later."

OPERATION SALVAGE

Kathie's mom called her room a "disaster area," and Kathie had to admit she had a point. So one weekend Kathie made plans to clean up the whole mess. To make the job easier—and more fun!—she invited her friend Susan to help out, with the understanding that they would work on Susan's room the next week.

The first thing they did was empty Kathie's closet. Out came all the clothes, shoes, belts, scarves and just plain junk. After they laid it all on the bed, Kathie sorted everything into four piles:

Category	Description	Destination
Perfect Clothes	Things Kathie wears a lot—they fit well, look good on her and are "ready to go" (no holes, broken heels, missing buttons, etc.).	Back into the closet.

Category	Description	Destination
Not-Quite-Perfect Clothes	Things that need to be mended or repaired.	Luckily there weren't too many of these. Kathie put them in the back of the closet, taking note of what had to be done to each one so she wouldn't forget about them.
Fine—But Not for Me	Clothes that Kathie hasn't worn for a long time because either they don't fit, she doesn't like them anymore or they aren't comfortable.	These go into boxes so that Kathie can either give them to someone else (maybe swap them with a friend) or donate them to charity.
No Good	Things that are worn out, or hopelessly damaged or stained.	These get thrown out.

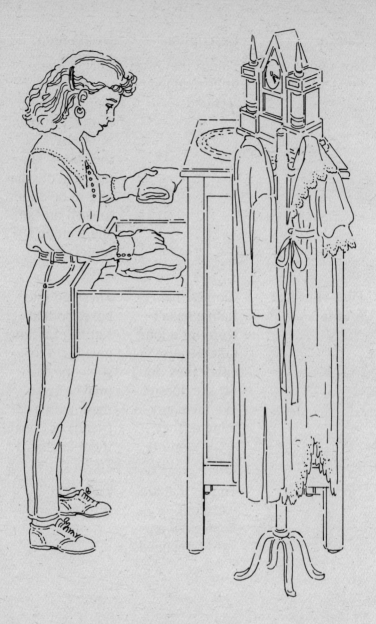

A little cleaning and organizing will go a long way in making your room feel like brand new.

When everything was put away, Kathie and Susan emptied Kathie's drawers. Into the trash bag went worn-out underwear, socks without mates and the T-shirt she hadn't worn in three years (that had holes in it besides). All the "good stuff" went back into the drawers—folded much more neatly, of course! But before they put the clothes back in the drawers, they added fresh sheets of drawer lining paper. These come in pretty colors and patterns and some are self-sticking. You can also buy perfumed ones, or dab your own favorite fragrance on cotton balls for your drawers—just be sure the wet cologne doesn't touch your clothes.

It was such a pleasure to see the clean closet and drawers that Kathie went on to organize her bookshelf and worktable, too. Out went the broken pencils, obsolete notes and discolored construction paper. Puzzles with missing pieces had to go, too. She put the toys and books she had outgrown into a box for the attic. A few favorite stuffed animals remained—she'd squeeze them in somewhere!

A little dusting helped, too. By the end of the day, Kathie's room already seemed like new. She could see everything in her closet, and it was all ready to wear. Her worktable/desk was neatly arranged with an empty space for writing or homework. Pens, pencils, scissors, paper clips and tape were right where she needed them. And the drawers were no longer crammed with jumbled items.

Cleaning up didn't solve every problem, of course. Kathie can still use a bit more hanging space in her closet and an extra shelf for her books, and she really wants some baskets or decorative boxes to store some of her hair ribbons and other accessories.

But at least now she can really *see* what she has—and plan what to do with it.

SOME ORGANIZING TIPS

Once you've gotten your belongings under control, how can you *keep* them that way? The best way is to make a place for everything and put things back when you're done with them. This is the old "a place for everything and everything in its place" idea—and it *does* work. Paints go back in the box, books go on the shelf, shoes go into the closet in pairs, your glasses go on the desk, and so on.

Try not to let the junk pile up. Get rid of old magazines, broken hair ornaments, old mail, wilted plants, etc. It's easier to prevent a big mess than to clean one up!

Make your bed when you get up—it only takes a minute and it makes your room look so much better. If you hate tucking a bedspread around pillows, you might try covering your bed with a comforter. Then, you can just straighten it out and plump up the pillows (in their matching shams) at the top.

THE TIME IS NOW

If you've been putting off a clean-up session, don't waste another day—do it now! Life is too precious to waste on chores that you can avoid by keeping your space in order. MESS leads to STRESS.

If you're having trouble getting in gear, think about these things: the pleasure of looking into a closet with only good-looking clothes that are all set to go (dressing will be a breeze!); the joy of finishing your homework on a neat work surface; the time you'll save if you don't have to look for things that are lost in the mess. Promise yourself a treat if you get it done: maybe some ice cream, or a new shirt or a piece of jewelry. Or maybe even something for your room!

A Place for Everything

*E*ven after a major "cleanup," you may find that you still need more storage—for clothes, books, hobbies, sports equipment and so on. Look around your room again: Do you have storage areas which you could do more with? Most people do. Read on to find out how to get the room you need from the space you already have.

THE MAGIC EXPANDING CLOSET

Nobody *ever* thinks their closet is big enough. But there are ways to make closets work better. Closet organizers found in variety stores and hardware stores can be really helpful. There are poles that can be hung from the rod that's already in your closet—to give you an extra, lower-hanging rod. If you have a grownup to help, you can also install extra rods.

You can add racks and boxes with compartments for shoes, sweaters and T-shirts. There are kits of sturdy cardboard pieces that you can assemble into drawers, boxes and shelves. Some of these boxes will slide under your bed.

With some thought and effort, you can even make your own closet organizers. Put a board across two piles of bricks (placed as far apart as the length of the board) and you have a shoe shelf for your closet floor. There's room under the board and on top of it for shoes and other items that can be stored flat. Paint the board or cover it with self-sticking paper.

HOLD-IT-ALL SHELVES

Shelves do a lot for a room—they hold books, games, puzzles, toys, dolls, stuffed animals, clay pieces and other collections. Shelves can also "grow up" with you. The same shelves that held alphabet books, pull toys and plastic blocks can later hold your soccer trophies, art supplies and your collection of mystery stories.

Extra shelf space is easy to get and holds all your favorite things from your books to art supplies to your precious collections.

If you can't afford a fancy bookcase or built-in shelves, maybe someone in your family is handy enough to install the kind of adjustable shelves that fit on wall brackets. Or you might buy an unfinished shelf unit at a store that sells unpainted furniture. You can paint the unit at home. Some people make shelves by laying painted boards on top of bricks—you can either leave the bricks as they are or spray-paint them interesting colors.

HOOKED ON YOU

Hooks come in all different shapes, sizes and colors. You can use them to hang colorful and attractive wall decorations. Hanging pretty things not only decorates your wall, it keeps items from getting tangled in drawers and closets and keeps them in sight when you need them. Some stores sell shelves with a row of pegs along the bottom—a good place to put hats, visors, jump ropes or a lightweight camera. Wall racks with pegs on them serve the same purpose.

You can put wall hooks almost anywhere. Put them inside your closet to hang things like strings of beads, belts, narrow scarves and hair ribbons. Or maybe you can hang them on a wall in the room—beside a dresser, closet door or table.

Do you have lots of heavy, bulky or different-sized items to store? Maybe your wall needs a pegboard with strong metal hooks on it. People use these pegboards in garages or workrooms because the hooks are strong enough for hanging tools. On these boards you could store sports equipment such as tied-together skates, tennis rackets and Frisbees, as well as photography equipment and other hobby supplies.

CREATIVE CONTAINERS

There are lots of other neat things you can use for storage. *Footlockers or trunks* at the foot of your bed will hold sweaters, bedding or out-of-season clothes. Trunks come in different metals as well as wood, wicker and straw. You can put a flat cushion or folded blanket across a strong trunk and use it as a seat.

Boxes of all shapes and sizes are good for holding all sorts of stuff. *Wooden crates or cardboard boxes* are handy, and can be painted or covered with self-sticking paper. The boxes come in many sizes for different objects—try using them to hold your sports equipment or art stuff. Boxes of the same size can be stacked. You could also use one to make your own wastebasket.

Old *hatboxes* from an attic or secondhand store, or new hatboxes made from kits you can buy at the sewing store (and cover with wallpaper or gift wrap) make great containers. These pretty boxes come in round or oval shapes with lids. You can use them in the closet, but some are too pretty to hide! Rhea has a stack of four in the corner of her room. They are different sizes with the largest on the bottom. The bottom box holds scarves, the second holds belts, the third holds jewelry and the top box holds her sewing gear.

And don't forget about *shoeboxes*. They can store all kinds of things. A row of shoeboxes the same size, covered with colors or a print that goes with your room, can neatly contain tubes of paint, paintbrushes, beads and strings to make jewelry, letters and Valentines that you want to save . . . just about any small item.

Baskets are great, too! They come in all kinds of shapes and sizes, and are nice-looking in natural straw, painted white, or with designs in different colors. You can build a room around pretty baskets, as ornaments that hang alone or hold flowers and plants. You can use them for wall storage, too. Decorate them with ribbons and dried flowers if you like frilly, feminine touches.

Jennifer had a clever idea. She found four inexpensive baskets in the five-and-dime store. Her dad put a fancy towel bar on her bedroom wall. Jennifer tied blue velvet ribbons on the white-painted baskets and tied them across the bar. They look super, and she has four containers for her colorful balls of yarn and needlework equipment.

A PLACE TO STUDY

Homework! Have you ever—ugh!—lost it? Forgotten to do it? Misplaced some important notes you needed to study for a test? For most of the year, school and homework are part of your routine. At home, you need a place and some basic equipment for studying and school assignments. Having a well-organized space and routine helps the work go more smoothly. If you get used to studying at certain times, in the same reliable place, with the things you have at hand, it can help raise your grades.

Do you have the equipment that you need for your study space? First on the list is a good light for reading and writing. It can be an overhead light or lamp directed onto the book or paper you are working on. A gooseneck lamp—the kind that has a movable head—is handy if you have a choice of lamps.

You also need a desk or table, for taking notes and doing other kinds of writing. Have you ever tried to write on a notebook that wobbles on your lap? It's difficult and comes out looking less than neat! Other materials are also helpful at study time—pens, pencils, erasers, notebook paper, your schoolbooks and a calendar or other kind of written schedule to remind you when assignments are due.

If you have a table or desk that's all yours for study, you can keep your materials on top of it, ready to go. But you might be doing your homework on a shared work surface or a table used for other activities by different family members. In this case, just put your materials into a sturdy container—a decorated cardboard box or a plastic bin from the drugstore or hardware store—and it will be ready to take to your study area.

If you can buy a brand-new desk, lucky you! But if you can't, remember that there are many ways to find a desk substitute. Remember some of the desk possibilities described in earlier chapters? You can try to find a secondhand desk or a good bargain.

You can look for a used school desk. Or you can make a desk out of painted plywood laid across two file cabinets. Formica boards or painted pieces of plywood can be laid across inexpensive storage cubes that you can buy in hardware or building-supply stores. Orange crates from a supermarket can also be painted and used as an inexpensive base for a homemade desk.

A table can work nicely, too. Jennifer made the top of her table special by having a piece of glass cut to fit the top. She put some of her favorite photographs around the edge like a border. If you don't have drawer space in a table desk, use desk-top accessories—either homemade or the kind sold in drugstores and variety stores. Many of these store-bought pieces can be put together in different ways to store whatever kinds of supplies you have. For example, there are "stacking units" that hold notebook or legal-sized notepads, and others for letters or pens.

THE EVER-HANDY BULLETIN BOARD

Do you already have one? If so, you know how useful it can be for hanging up lists, reminder notes and other important pieces of paper. You can also use it to display small decorative items: greeting cards, stickers, dried flowers and so on.

Where's the best place for a friendly bulletin board? Putting it by a desk or study area is ideal—you can use it to organize study plans, too. If you share a room, it can be used as a room divider. If you share a bulletin board, put colored tape or a ribbon straight down the middle to divide it. Each side can be labeled with the owner's name or initials.

Want to try making your own bulletin board? Look in attics and stores for a picture frame that fits your taste and the style of your room. Cut a piece of thick corrugated cardboard (the kind used to make shipping boxes) to the size of the frame. Cover it with pretty colored felt and tape the felt across the back. Attach the cardboard to the frame with push pins.

You can also make a bulletin board without a frame. Just wrap a piece of felt around some cardboard and staple it on the back. You can glue a border of ribbon around all the edges and use the ribbon to hang the bulletin board on the wall.

A COZY CORNER

Do you like to read in a comfortable spot? Maybe you would enjoy having a "cozy corner" in your room. You can make one by putting a small fluffy rug over a large pillow or cushion. (Or use a beanbag chair.) Then add some other pillows to cuddle up with and maybe a small soft blanket.

Janet made a cozy corner out of an old sofa cushion her aunt planned to throw away. Janet's room is decorated in green and white so she and her mom covered the sofa cushion with a green flannel sheet that they found on sale in a variety store. They added some pillows with covers in different shades of green. Janet used a white afghan as a "throw" to make the corner extra-cozy for reading and sewing. She had a small bookcase, so she moved it to enclose one side of her corner.

Pat made a reading corner from a rusty-orange beanbag chair and some flower-print cushions. She covered the beanbag in canvas fabric, and the pillows in shiny cotton chintz, so the textures made an appealing contrast. Pat knows how to sew, so she is making a small patchwork quilt to use in the corner.

JUST FOR YOU

By now, your room should be much better organized, with more room for storage, studying, sleeping, resting and reading. Do you have other activities that require unusual equipment?

Are you a budding ballerina? Not many people can have a practice barre in their room, but a towel rack installed on one area of free wall space can give you a place to bend and stretch!

If you are an exercise nut you'll need an area of open space on the floor so that you can work out. You might have to move things around a bit when you exercise. When shopping for furniture, look for folding pieces, like chairs, tables, easels and so on. (These are helpful if you do any activity that requires floor space.)

Collectors will have to be clever with wall and shelf space. If space is limited, you may have to rotate parts of your collection, so that certain pieces are on display while others are either stored or placed at the back of the shelf. Remember that hanging baskets in different shapes can be very useful for storage. Large bulletin boards or groups of bulletin boards can show off artwork or card collections.

It may be hard getting organized and finding workable space for everything in your room. But the rewards are great, too. In the long run, you'll save time—time you can use to do things that are more pleasant than looking frantically for that lost math homework!

In Search of Style

*A*s you make plans and begin decorating your room, you'll probably find yourself dealing with questions of "style." You'll find you particularly like certain furniture and colors. One room in a magazine or department store appeals to you—another doesn't. Each girl has her own likes and dislikes and ways of doing things—that's her style. Your personal style can help make your room really special and entirely different from anybody else's.

Of course, you also have to ask whether the "dream room" you have in mind will really fit the

Making a scrapbook of your dream rooms using pictures cut from magazines can help you find your own sparkling style.

way you live, day by day. For example, you might love lace and white eyelet, and pastel colors for the walls and carpets, but some compromises may be in order if you walk in every evening with muddy track shoes—or if your hobby is oil painting.

Finding out more about decorating styles will help you figure out what your room really needs—and it's fun. Some girls keep a file or scrapbook with decorating ideas. They clip magazine and catalogue pictures of furniture, color combinations and room styles that they like. They jot down interesting ideas and save articles that tell how to make pillows and other things for their rooms.

By looking through your scrapbook or idea file, you can learn more about your style. You'll notice that you seem to choose certain colors and kinds of furniture over and over and over again. You'll find that some rooms make you feel comfortable or happy and others don't.

Still wondering about your style? Take this quiz to learn more:

☆☆   WHAT'S MY STYLE QUIZ   ☆☆

For all quizzes, please write your answers on a separate piece of paper.

1. *If I could pick a new bed (and the sky's the limit!), I'd like:*
   a. A modern style with a simple shape.
   b. A frilly bed with pastel or flowery sheets— and I'd love a canopy!
   c. An old-fashioned Early American style, with a brass or wood headboard.

d. Something really different—maybe a brightly painted headboard or no headboard at all—and wild designs on the bedspread!

2. *My favorite colors are*:
   a. Clear bright colors, sometimes black and white.
   b. Soft pastels.
   c. Medium shades of rust-red, blue, cream, brown, grass-green or gold.
   d. Colors that are "different"—purple, fuchsia, turquoise or deep coral.

3. *My favorite ways to spend time in my room are*:
   a. Listening to the latest hit songs.
   b. Writing—in my diary or to a pen pal—and putting photographs in my album.
   c. Working on my knitting or hooked rug; practicing the flute.
   d. Practicing dances from jazz class; painting abstract pictures.

4. *The things I'd like most for my room are*:
   a. A great stereo and headphones.
   b. A pretty bookcase to hold my favorite books and my doll collection.
   c. A rocking chair with a cushion in my favorite colors.
   d. An easel and art stand for painting.

5. *My favorite classes and activities include*:
   a. Math or science class; trying out for musicals and plays.
   b. Reading, writing compositions; ballet class.
   c. Sports—playing and watching; crafts.

d. Art, jazz dancing, studying modern poetry.
6. *My favorite kind of book is*:
   a. Science fiction; math puzzles.
   ~b. *Little Women*, others by Louisa May Alcott; *The Secret Garden*.
   c. Horse stories like *Misty of Chincoteague;* biographies.
   d. Unusual poetry, books about art and artists.
7. *My desk or work table is*:
   a. Pretty well organized with a stack of magazines in one corner and some beads that I'm making into bracelets.
   b. Kind of cluttered with photos, letters, a container for potpourri and some fresh flowers or plants.
   ~c. Made out of wood with some brass or pewter containers for pens and stuff; my collection of glass animals runs across the back.
   d. Something I designed myself out of black and white painted plywood boxes and a dark red board; my sketchbooks and poetry books are on top.

After you finish, add up the number of a's, b's, c's and d's that you've marked. Do you have more of one letter than the others?

If you checked mostly a's, then you are a *"modern girl."*

If you checked mostly b's, then you are a *"romantic girl."*

If you checked mostly c's, then you are a *"traditional girl."*

If you checked mostly d's, then you are an *"artistic girl."*

☆☆☆

FOR MODERN GIRLS

Modern girls have trendy tastes—they like the latest rock groups and know the newest dances and clothing styles. If you are this type, you might feel most at home in a room that has a modern look: simple lines in furniture and curtains, a plain-colored carpet—maybe with an area rug in a bright contrasting color or with a modern design (wide stripes or a mixture of colors).

You might want to plan a color scheme like black and white with accents in a bright color such as red, sapphire blue, emerald green or sunshine yellow. You could try making your bed into a sofa by day (see Chapter Eight for more details). You probably won't want lots of frills or pastels in your room, or an old-fashioned rocker or wooden furniture with fancy carving.

You will probably want a room that has space for all your various interests—shelves to hold records or cassette tapes, closet hooks or shelves for the up-to-date accessories you like to add to your wardrobe. (Maybe a tray on your dresser to hold a collection of sunglasses?) Stick with light-colored wood or plastic furniture that can be arranged in different ways.

If you have to work with furniture that is not your style, you can add your own special touches—

posters of your favorite singers, pillows in your favorite colors or modern graphic or stencil designs on the wall.

FUN AND FRILLS

Romantic types are real flowers-and-lace kinds of girls. They enjoy pretty, girlish touches in the clothes they wear and the way they decorate their rooms. If you are a romantic type, you probably prefer pastel colors and flowery prints. These touches can make a very pretty and restful room. And you'll have dozens of lovely sheets and bedcovers to choose from—lots of fabric designers like the same kinds of colors and prints that you do!

Be careful not to make the room so fancy and delicate that it is hard to keep clean. The frilly bed linens you pick should be easy to care for. Lacy pillow covers should be removable for easy laundering.

DAINTY DETAILS

✪ A small pastel area rug from a variety store. (These inexpensive small rugs come in pastel stripes and flowered designs.)
✪ A wallpaper border with a pastel floral design.
✪ An eyelet dust ruffle, if you use a comforter on the bed.

What other special touches can you add to a room that's already done in a style that may not be "you"?

A row of lace or eyelet can dress up the edges of pillows, bedspreads and curtains. Jamie gave her plain white window shades a new look by sewing pastel-colored bows on them in a scattered design. Just a few stitches at the back of each bow did the trick. You could also tie back plain curtains with wide satin bows made from yards of pastel ribbon bought at a fabric store.

TRADITIONAL TOUCHES

Traditional girls feel most at home in an old-fashioned room—one with lots of warm-toned woods, a braided rag rug and a bed with a patchwork quilt on top. If you are a traditional type and already have that kind of furniture, you're set, but if you have to work with other styles in the pieces you already have, never fear. You can probably make changes with color. Traditional rooms are often decorated in soothing medium tones, such as medium shades of rust-red, blue, cream, brown, grass-green or gold.

You won't see modern steel furniture or lime green and hot pink in a traditional room! What you *will* find are things like rocking chairs, roll-top desks, paintings of horses and country scenes, samplers, patchwork quilts, striped wallpaper and objects made of pewter and china.

TRADITIONAL TRIMMINGS

✪ Frame some photographs in inexpensive wood or "pewter-look" frames for your desk.

✪ Pick a traditional striped wallpaper if you have a choice.

✪ Use traditional color combinations like these: dusty blue with rust and cream, bottle green with peach and ivory, antique gold with brown muted orange.

✪ A braided rug or rag rug (check those attics again, as well as yard sales, secondhand stores and variety stores).

✪ Wall ideas include framed pictures of birds, flowers or horses; an old sampler, if your family has one; or a silhouette picture (black paper cutouts mounted on off-white paper and framed) that you can make yourself.

✪ Patchwork quilts are the ultimate traditional trimming, and, if you really feel ambitious, you can make one yourself! You can learn how by reading a book from the library or by asking an experienced quilter to help you. Sewing a patchwork quilt takes some time and effort, but the results will be very special when you see your own handmade quilt spread across your bed!

ART FOR ART'S SAKE

Artistic girls are very individual in their tastes and style. If you are this type, you probably like unusual colors and decorating ideas, and your room will reflect your preferences.

Be careful not to get so wild in your color schemes and furniture that the room is too exciting to sleep in. Tone down "hot" colors with some restful areas of white, beige or other "quiet" colors. Keep your artistic hobbies under control with a careful storage plan or else your room will never look like anything but a mess!

Try to find an easel in a thrift shop or ask to receive one as a gift. Then you can put your latest work of art on it and it will be a focal point in the room. You may want to have a corkboard to display other artwork, or poems you have written.

Like the modern girl, you may do something different with your bed—remove the headboard if you have one; turn the bed into something that looks more like a sofa. If you can't change the colors in your room, you may be able to add pillow covers or curtain trim in the colors you love. Most of all, just remember that decorating a room is an artistic endeavor, so give it your artistic all!

THE BEST OF ALL WORLDS

Did you check a combination of different letters? You can combine the things you like from different styles—just make sure they look good together. For example, straw baskets or trunks can be used with most styles; so can wicker. Plain wood or white-painted shelves go with most rooms. A touch of lace may be fine with Early American settings or more modern rooms.

Be careful not to be too extreme, though. A super-modern graphic design in bright colors might "throw off" the look of a room full of patchwork and traditional furniture. You should also consider the size of the furniture you use, especially in a small room. Large, heavy pieces may overwhelm a small space. Light wicker or transparent pieces may work better. Your own eye and the opinion of your friends and parents can help you to judge what things blend well together.

Finding furniture and accessories that suit your taste, your budget and the space you have to work with can be a challenge. Use these guidelines to plan a room that expresses "you"—and let your creativity lead the way.

Color Your Room Wonderful

*C*olor, pattern and texture are three of the most important things to think about when decorating. Finding the best balance of these three in your room might take some practice, but it's vital. And it can be fun, too!

EVERYWHERE YOU LOOK

Colors! We are surrounded by them everywhere we go. Just look around you. Think about all the things in your room that have a color:

- *Paint and/or wallpaper*
- *Fabrics on bed and other furniture*
- *Rugs, carpets and other floor coverings*
- *Curtains*
- *Accessories*
- *Everything!*

Colors affect our moods as well. Sometimes by association: Picture a summer garden filled with different shades of green leaves and colorful flowers. Or a country road in autumn—leaves drenched in warm oranges, rusts, golds and reds. Even wearing certain colors can affect our mood. How do you feel when you wear red or hot pink? Is it a different feeling you get from a white T-shirt and a pair of bleached jeans?

Colors are a fun part of decorating and a key part of personal style. One of the best things about color is the way it "lifts" a room for a low cost. (After all, you pay the same price for paint in an upbeat color you love as you would for the same type of paint in a dreary shade.)

COMBINING COLORS

Which colors do *you* like? Lights and brights? Blacks and whites? Neutral earth tones? Do you like warm colors or cool ones? Deep jewel tones or pastels? Deciding what colors you want in your room can be tricky. You're going to be living with these colors—maybe for several years. Think about rooms that you like a lot: What colors are used to decorate *them*?

If you are keeping a scrapbook or decorating file, browse through it. Do certain colors keep popping up, over and over? Are they sunny yellows, oranges and reds? Are they cool blues, greens and violets? Are they dark or light tints? What color combinations do you like better than others?

Color chips from a paint store can help, too. There are dozens of shades of every color. If you're planning to paint your room, you can take the chips home and think about which ones you like best. You can try arranging the chips in different combinations.

Some people use the seasons to choose colors and combinations. Here's a list of some colors that the seasons bring to mind:

FALL	WINTER
copper	icy white
orange	icy blue
rust	icy pink
russet-red	icy lilac
olive green	ruby red
warm beige	sapphire
brown	pine
	black

SPRING	SUMMER
peach	light navy blue
sky blue	medium blue
ivory	medium pink
grass green	rose
yellow	periwinkle blue
golden tan	emerald green
aqua	lilac

The colors in these groupings often go together well. Did you find several colors in the lists that you wear a lot? Colors that you look good in will probably also be appealing when used to decorate your room.

Still feeling puzzled about your "color style"? Here's a work sheet to help you learn more:

☆☆ COLOR WORK SHEET ☆☆

1. *A look through my closet shows mostly:*
    - a. Bright clear shades—red, yellow, blue, green.
    - b. Neutrals and earth tones—white, black, brown, gray, beige.
    - c. Soft sherbety pastels—pink, sky blue, peach, mint, aqua.
    - d. Dark dramatic colors—burgundy, violet, teal, deep coral.

2. *When I picture my ideal room, it is decorated in this (these) color(s):* _____
3. *These things come to mind when I think of the following colors:*

red	orange
green	black
yellow	pink
brown	white
purple	blue

4. *When I wear* _____ *I get lots of compliments.*
5. *The color(s) in my room right now that I like best is (are):* _____ .
6. *The color(s) in my room right now that I like least is (are):* _____ .
7. *The color(s) that I find most relaxing is (are):* _____ .
8. *My favorite colors are:*
   A. The cool colors—blue, violet, green and "icy" pastel tones.
   B. The warm colors—red, yellow, orange.
9. *I especially like:*
   A. Soft tones.
   B. Bright tones.
10. *If I could buy four new T-shirts or sweaters, they would be in these colors:* _____

☆☆☆

Look at your answers and think about what you've learned so far. If you're planning to change your room color or add a new color to it, read on so that your color choices will make your room perfect for *you*.

COLOR AFFECTS THE SPACE

Besides your own color preferences, you'll want to think about how color affects the other features in your room. Is the room dark (not exposed to much sunlight)? Using a light, bright paint color will cheer it up. Is the room very light (exposed to bright sun)? You can "cool it" by using light blues, sea greens, lavender or mauve. What colors are in the rest of your home? If you want to have a bright green room and the rest of the house or apartment is pale blue and rose, you may have to find a way for your room to "blend in"—at least a bit—with the other rooms.

Liza found herself in this last situation: Her mom's decorating colors were olive green, muted gold and burnt orange and Liza wanted pink in her room. Their solution? Liza's room has the same muted gold carpet as the rest of the bedrooms, but they found flower-printed fabric to make curtains and a bedspread. The print has Liza's pink, a dab of the gold and even some green in the leaves and flowers. This allows Liza to use pink in many accessories around her room, while still allowing her room to fit in with the rest of the house.

Paint can be used to change the size of a room. Light shades tend to open up a room; dark colors can make it seem smaller. If you love dark colors but have a small space to work with, you could use your favorites in the accent pieces: pillows, throws, or artwork. Using the same paint on walls, doors and woodwork may also make the room look more spacious.

Give the room a harmonious look by using the same color in more than one place. For example, if you paint an accent wall behind your bed in jade green, use other touches of jade green around your room—in a pillow, in a print, as tiebacks for the curtains. Bright, intense colors attract attention so use them only where you want the eye to go. You can also get a nice effect by using different tones of a single color all over the room.

Two-color combinations can also give you a great look. As a general rule, work with no more than three main colors, especially in a small room, so that it has a "tied-together" look. Some ideas for "three-color combos" are also below:

COLOR COMBINATIONS

Two Colors	*Three Colors*
clear white and bright blue	mocha brown, sunny orange and ivory
peach pink and celery green	sky blue, sun gold and grass green
banana yellow and aquamarine	sky blue, coral and lemon yellow
sky blue and melon	white, royal blue and true red
lemon yellow and geranium pink	white, pale lemon yellow and powder blue
scarlet and pearl gray	navy blue, burgundy and cream
forest green and ivory	white, grass green and sky blue
	red, white and black
	pale pink, white and emerald green

OTHER COLOR-PICKING TRICKS

You can find your color "scheme" from something that is already in your room . . . or from something that you can plan to put there.

It works like this: Suppose your carpet is a certain color and you have to use it. You'll have to think about what shades go with the carpet, as well as what colors are your favorites. Maybe you'll be able to buy new sheets and curtains in a print that combines the carpet color with the colors you love.

Maybe you have something in your room that you really like such as a patterned rug, some curtains or sheets, or an upholstered chair. If so, you can build a color scheme around that one piece. Pick a light color from it for the wall paint. Use other colors in plain or patterned sheets and curtain fabrics, as well as accent pieces—pillows, chair cushions, wastebaskets, artwork and desk accessories.

SMART PATTERNS

A sure-fire way to help a room look "together" is through mixing and matching patterns. Patterns can really add sparkle to a room and give it an individual touch.

It's a lot like planning an outfit. Say you're wearing jeans. You add a white turtleneck and red V-neck sweater. What's missing? Pattern! You look fine, but you could pep up your outfit with something like a pair of red and white dotted socks or a paisley scarf that picks up the red of your sweater or maybe a striped headband or a flowered vest.

At the same time, if you added all *four* of these printed accessories, you might hear a few comments about "that girl who looks like she got dressed in the dark." Similarly, patterns used in a clumsy way can defeat a room. Just imagine how dizzy you'd get in a room where everything was covered with a different print—a room full of dots, stripes, flowers, geometrics, plaids and so on!

Some patterns combine better than others. A small thin stripe can go with a floral print, for example, if the colors go together. Dots and stripes might look nice together, too. The colors in the prints can tie different patterns together.

If you have a bright, boldly patterned area such as a wall hanging, a bedspread or an upholstered chair, you might want to let that be the main "focus" in the room. Use smaller, less showy patterns (like stripes) or solids elsewhere. Patterns draw attention to themselves—the bolder the pattern and the larger the area it covers, the more it grabs your attention.

As a rule, smaller rooms can use fewer patterns and smaller types of patterns than larger rooms can. But using the same pattern all over—in sheets, pillows, curtains and wallpaper—sometimes works well in a small room.

PATTERNED ON SUCCESS

Here are some examples of rooms that use patterns in appealing ways:

Casey's room: Casey has powder-blue carpeting and a patterned floral area rug (the rug has powder blue, rose and muted brown on a cream background). Her walls are pink with a floral border near

A brightly patterned quilt or bedspread can help pull your room "together."

the ceiling (colors: pink, powder blue and light yellow on white). Her sheets are white with a pink tulip design; her quilt is powder blue with thin pink and white stripes. Her curtains are white.

Angie and Sue's room: They found sheets and wallpaper in coordinating prints for their room. The wallpaper and curtains are made from a yellow, peach and green plaid. Two pillows are the same. Two other pillows have yellow and green stripes; so do the sheets. The bedspread is reversible—striped on one side with big yellow flowers on the other.

Rita's room: The floor is wood with an area rug in dark blue and white. The sheets are blue and white paisley; the quilt has multicolored blocks in large geometric shapes. The walls are white; the curtains are plain blue with white trim. A rocking chair in the corner has a white cushion with a star design in different shades of blue.

Caroline's room: The walls are white with sunny yellow trim. The wall behind the bed has sunny yellow wallpaper with very small flowers in pink and blue with green vines. The sheets are yellow and the comforter has a yellow, light blue, white and peachy pink floral stripe design. The cotton area rug on the floor is pale yellow with thin woven stripes of light blue, peachy pink and mint green.

TEXTURE ADDS APPEAL

Like color, texture is all around us. Texture is the surface look of an object and also the way it feels—smooth and rough are two good examples. Fabrics can be satiny, velvety, nubby, flannelly or slippery.

They can have a similar appearance all over or be irregular, like burlap, raw silk or linen. As with patterns, a touch of texture in your space adds eye appeal. It might be the touch that turns your space into something really special.

Start by looking around the room again. How many different kinds of textures—very rough, rough, flat-textured, smooth or ultra-smooth—can you find? If most of the things in the room have about the same texture, all rough or nubby—corduroy, flannel, burlap or velveteen—you might want to add a little shine.

GLOSSY AND GLAMOROUS

- Mirrors.
- Artwork or photos framed in glass or shiny frames.
- Fabrics like satin, taffeta, silk-like polyester or cotton chintz.
- Polished wood surfaces.
- Wood furniture or accessories painted with high-gloss paint or enamel.
- Shiny metal objects, such as picture frames or metal lamps or bed frames.
- Things made of glass, crystal, china, ceramic or foil paper.
- Transparent or shiny plastic.
- Shiny green plants.

Again, think about the style of the room, your own tastes, and how well things go together. Transparent plastic may not work in a room that is old-fashioned in every other way. And maybe you really want a soft, non-shiny look in the room. So, just a touch of shine—brass containers or plants with shiny green leaves, for instance, may be all you need to perk things up.

On the other hand, what if your room is full of very smooth textures—with shiny, slippery fabrics, glossy paint on the walls, polished wood and metal, foil wallpaper, crystal lamps, or glitter-trimmed penholders? You might want to tone it down—it will give your eyes a rest and give *you* more of a chance to shine.

A TOUCH OF ROUGH (OR FURRY)

- Bleached unpolished wood furniture.
- Flat-finished paint on walls or wood furniture and accessories.
- Fabrics with a bumpy or furry weave: corduroy, velveteen, burlap, fake suede, felt.
- Wicker or straw objects.
- Cork on walls or a bulletin board.
- Carpeting, woven or grass area rugs, hooked rugs.
- Woven or knitted things—wool afghans, mohair throws, needlepoint.
- Furry things—like stuffed teddy bears!

Just remember that the important thing is balance. So, mix and match, and if you use your eye as a judge, your room will end up with the perfect combination of textures.

Not Just Scenery

Walls, floors and windows—sometimes these areas fade into the background of a room. Don't let them! They are important parts of the overall look: They "set the stage" and can give you a color or decorating theme to work with. And if they aren't too terrific and can't be changed, you can spruce them up or downplay them in clever ways.

Let's start with your walls. Are they dreary or dynamite? Maybe they just got a fresh coat of paint in your favorite color, or you've wallpapered them recently. But if not, there are loads of things you can do.

PAINTING POSSIBILITIES

You already know how much you can improve a dreary room just by painting the walls. But have you thought about painting the walls different colors? In a long rectangular room, you can paint the two farthest walls a deeper color than the two other facing walls (plum with mauve, for example). Or how about painting the wall behind your bed one color and the other three walls a different color? This works particularly well in a wide room.

How about painting patterns on one or more walls? You can use masking tape to lay out stripes. You can even mark out a plaid if you are clever with a paintbrush. Ruthie decided to paint a row of flowers on one wall. She painted a bed of green grass near the floor and added tulips in joyful shades of red, yellow and coral. You can make a freeform design of colored waves—try picking three different colors and using small rollers to paint wavy lines between two doors in the room, for example. Other girls have designed rainbows, clouds or stars.

If you are not so handy with a paintbrush, you might try a stencil kit to paint designs on your wall or in a border near the ceiling. Stencils are very popular, and cost less than wallpaper. Follow the directions in the stencil kit or instruction book carefully. You'll need to buy paint and a brush with rather short, stiff bristles if the kit doesn't include them. Be sure to tape the stencil securely on the wall area to be painted. After you finish painting, you should let the paint dry until it is at the "tacky" stage—not too wet (or it will smear) and not too dry (pieces of the design could crack off with the stencil)—before removing the stencil.

You can even get letter stencils and add your initials to a piece of painted furniture, a headboard or a wall to show "whose side is whose" in a shared room. By following directions and/or working with an experienced older person, you'll come up with a unique look for your walls!

IF YOU'RE BUYING WALLPAPER . . .

If the family budget allows, you may decide to wallpaper your room. Wallpapers come in many styles and colors. When choosing the paper, you should consider the size of your room. If your room is small, a large, bold print might overwhelm it. In a small room you can get a nice, harmonious effect by using the same print everywhere—on bedding, walls and curtains. On the other hand, a teensy pastel stripe might not do much for a large room, so try those bolds.

Give a thought to using wallpaper on only one wall. You can put stripes or flowers behind the bed, for instance. This wall will be the "spotlight" area or focal point of the room.

You can also add texture to a room with wallpaper. Some wallpaper has a metallic or texture finish instead of a printed all-over design. Papers called "grass-cloth" look like rough linen or burlap fabric and go well with many styles of furniture.

Suppose you love wallpaper, but it costs too much money? Some stores and mail-order services sell wall-paper at discount prices. And paint and wallpaper stores often have "reduced price" bins, like the fabric stores do. These bins contain rolls that people have returned to the store unused. They also have leftover rolls of paper designs that have been "discontinued"—they are no longer being made. These rolls are some-times reduced 50% or more in price.

Keep in mind what was said earlier about style and color. When you're looking at a paper in a store ask yourself if it goes with the overall style and color scheme of the room. In other words, if you have a traditional room done in browns and tans, bringing home a hot pink and black wallpaper (which hap-pens to be on sale) is probably not a good idea. Stores will usually let you bring home a sample of the paper so that you can check it in your room.

FABRIC WALL HANGINGS

Instead of covering a wall with patterned paper, you may decide to add patterns with a fabric "painting" on one or more walls. You can find all kinds of designs at fabric stores to make different-sized wall hangings for your room. Consider some of the possibilities: a pattern in sand and rust tones that looks like a Native American rug; bold geomet-ric prints in purples, teal blues or black and white for an up-to-the-minute look; flowers in dainty pastels or bright modern colors; fruit prints; wavy stripes; animal prints; or scenic designs for a fabric mural.

One way to hang the fabric is to use wood stretcher bars—the kind that artists use for their canvases. You can buy sets of bars, in different sizes, at an art supply store. They are easy to put together and will make frames in different sizes—16" x 20", 18" x 24", 20" x 24", 20" x 30" and larger. If you are using this method, pick out the fabric first so that you know how wide it is. You will need to allow about three inches of extra fabric all around to wrap the edges around the four sides of the wood frame.

After you've picked your fabric and decided what size hanging you want, buy the bars to make the frame—two matching pieces each for the length and the width. Here's how to make the wall hanging:

Quick Fabric Art

1. Iron the fabric to get wrinkles out.
2. Cut it to about the right size, allowing several extra inches all around. Make sure that the part of the design that you want is in the right place before you cut!
3. Lay the fabric *right side down* on your work surface.
4. Put the frame *right side down* on the fabric.
5. As a test, use tacks to attach the fabric. Pull the fabric around the back of the frame evenly. First tack down the middle of one side, then the middle of the opposite side. Do the same thing on the two remaining sides. Then add other tacks on both sides of every corner.

6. Turn it over and check—is the design where you want it? (This is not a problem if your fabric has an all-over pattern). If not, readjust and check again.
7. Staple the fabric, using the same method you used to tack it. As you staple, pull the fabric firmly but not very tight. If you pull too tightly, the fabric threads will get out of line. Remove the tacks.
8. When you're done, cut excess fabric from the back of the frame. If the fabric seems too loose, spray it lightly with water. It will shrink a bit when it dries.
9. Hang this kind of "painting" the same way that you hang framed artwork—by attaching a picture wire across the back and hanging it on a picture hook on the wall.

Another way to make a fabric wall hanging is to hang it on decorative rods or "dowels"—two matching pieces of wood or plastic that are inserted in openings called "casings" along the top and bottom of the fabric. You can buy them at fabric and craft stores.

Here's how to make this kind of fabric hanging:

Quicker Fabric Art

1. Buy a piece of fabric long enough to make a rod casing at the top and bottom.
2. Sew hems on the two sides of the fabric.

Fabric wall hangings are cheap and easy to make and you decide exactly what colors and patterns will brighten up your room.

3. To make the casing, sew a deep hem at the top and bottom, either by hand or with a sewing machine. The size of your casing will depend upon what size rods you are using.
4. Insert your rods or dowels.
5. Tie the ends of a cord or strong ribbon on the ends of the top rod. Hang the cord on the wall from its middle, so that the cord has a triangle shape over the hanging.

POSTERS, POSTCARDS AND MORE

If you prefer plain painted walls, or you just can't afford fancy papers and fabrics, your walls can still look great! There are dozen of ways to dress them up. Posters are a great way to liven up a room. They come in many sizes and have pictures of sports heroes, musicians, film stars, famous artworks and historic and beautiful places.

If your parents are worried that your collection of posters or other artwork will ruin the paint or plaster on the walls, tell them about a product sold at drugstores and five-and-dime stores that will hang your posters safely. It comes in small packages, under different brand names, and looks like chunks of clay or gum. Ask the salesclerk for help, if you have trouble finding it. It's easy to use: You simply break off tiny pieces, then use them to stick your posters on the wall. It is less damaging to paint and wallpaper than nails or tape.

You can display other things in this manner as

well. For example, a collection of postcards can be put directly on the wall or you can attach them to long ribbons and hang the ribbons vertically on the wall. Maps work well as posters, too. You can find nice ones in magazines that people have stored in the attic or are planning to discard. Travel posters are nice, too, and you might be able to get them free at a travel agency or auto club office—ask for maps there, too.

Collages make nice wall decorations. You can make collages of pictures, greeting cards, seashells, buttons, snapshots . . . pretty much anything! There are books that tell how to make different kinds of collages. Many use pictures cut out of magazines. Annie decided to make a collage of her own name from letters in newspapers and magazines. Sometimes, she even found the name "Annie" spelled out. She glued the letters and words on a large sheet of black construction paper, put it in an inexpensive pink drugstore frame and hung it over her bed. It's original and very personal!

Mirrors and mirror tiles can make any space seem larger. Mirror tiles come in squares that can be stuck on the walls, if your parents agree. If you put a mirror on your wall, consider putting it where it reflects a view or something else you like.

Try making your own artificial wreath. You can get the basics from a crafts store and decorate it yourself with artificial flowers, ribbons, etc. Hana got a plain wreath for the wall above her bed. She had the clever idea of decorating it to suit the season or upcoming holiday. In February, it was covered with red hearts; in July, she attached little paper flags . . . and so on through the year.

Here are some more ideas for pepping up your walls:

- ✪ *Your own artwork.*
- ✪ *A wall full of decorative paper fans.*
- ✪ *Your favorite poems, illustrated by you and written in your best handwriting with colorful felt-tip pens. (Mount them on colorful construction paper for a "finished" look.)*
- ✪ *Plain baskets or baskets full of dried flowers or seashells.*
- ✪ *Your hat collection hanging on pegs.*
- ✪ *Pressed leaves and flowers, framed.*
- ✪ *A favorite jigsaw puzzle, framed.*
- ✪ *A wall of cork tiles that can hold your artwork, maps or cards.*
- ✪ *Record album covers arranged in straight rows, diagonally or in other patterns on the wall.*
- ✪ *Borders around the top of the wall near the ceiling made of designs from self-sticking paper (the kind used for lining shelves and drawers).*

You can make your own "frames" for pretty much anything, by attaching ribbon or colored tape around the edges of pictures or artwork. With these ideas and some of your own, you should soon have happier walls!

WHAT'S UNDER YOUR FEET?

Look down as you step into your room. You may be seeing wall-to-wall carpet or a floor covered with tile, wood or linoleum. Could your floor use a "lift"? Whatever floor you have, you can do something with it.

78

A plush wall-to-wall carpet in your favorite color would be nice, of course. So would a beautifully patterned area rug or gleaming wood floor in A-1 condition. But most of us will have to settle for more modest floor coverings.

First on the "floor improvement list" is to clean up what you have. Ask your parents about getting some rug shampoo if your carpet needs spot removal or "freshening up." A careful cleaning can make a big difference. If you have wood, tile or linoleum, you can scrub that, too, and apply some wax if your parents agree.

Now take another look. Is your carpet worn out in one or more places? Try arranging furniture over the worn spots, or cover them with an inexpensive area rug from a discount or variety store. Some bathroom rugs are attractive and don't cost much money.

Do you know how to make a hooked rug, or do you know someone who can teach you? Some girls buy rug kits at fabric or craft stores to add their own special touch to the floor. It's a good project for those quiet winter nights when you're watching television. You can also make a patchwork rug to add a colorful accent to your room.

Patchwork Rug

You will need:

- ✪ Scraps of different-colored carpet. (Try collecting carpet pieces from family and friends, or from a carpet store that will give you the pieces they plan to discard.)

- A piece of burlap fabric about the size of the rug you plan to make.
- Strong scissors.
- Double-faced carpet tape.
- A large piece of paper the size of the rug you want to make.

To make the rug:

1. Lay the carpet pieces out on a large piece of paper and move them around into a design that you like. Trace the outline of the rug on the paper and cut it out.
2. Use the paper pattern to cut the burlap into the right shape, leaving about three inches on each side for a hem.
3. Tape the pieces to the burlap with two-sided carpet tape.
4. Hem the edges of the burlap.
5. Put the rug down and enjoy!

Some stores sell inexpensive rugs woven of jute, hemp, sisal or straw. These come in natural tones or colors. They work nicely in modern-looking rooms and can give a "tropical look" when used with lots of leafy green plants.

If you have a wood or linoleum floor and your parents say it's okay, you can paste some stick-on flowers on it, or stick on other designs that you cut from rolls of self-sticking shelf-liner paper.

What if your floor is just plain ugly and you can't cover it up? Then the trick is to draw attention *away* from the floor and onto the walls, bed or windows—whatever part of the room you like best.

HOW'S THE VIEW?

Whether you have one window or six to decorate, you need to think about three things: privacy, light control and the view. First, ask yourself if you need a window covering at all. If you live in a house surrounded by fifty farm acres, privacy isn't going to be much of an issue, but light control may be. You should be able to let sunshine in during the day, and darken the room for sleeping at night. If you have a lovely view, you should try to play it up as much as possible.

One way to control light and gain privacy is to use shades alone or combine them with light curtains. Inexpensive vinyl roller shades are sold at hardware and variety stores. They come in white and other colors and in different widths, and they aren't too difficult to install.

If you already have these roller shades (or plan to buy them), you can sew or glue something on the bottom: fringe, rickrack, lace, an eyelet ruffle or braid trim. Using more than one row of trimming will give you a fancier effect. (Note: You can also put these kinds of trims on plain curtains or cloth shades.) Painting designs on the shades with an alkyd, flat-finish paint—or cutting designs from self-sticking paper and pressing them on the rolled-out shade—can change your shades from dull and drab to fabulous. You can also use a stencil kit from the craft store to add hearts, stars, flowers and so on.

You could also cover your shades with low-cost self-sticking paper (the kind that is used to line shelves) from the variety store or drugstore. Suppose your room is red, yellow and blue? You could find a plaid paper with those colors to cover your shades.(You might need some help to hold the shades flat while you cover them with paper.)

Do your shades have pull-strings? Give them a special touch by attaching pretty bells or some strings of beads or crystals, a cluster of ribbon bows to match the room or a tassel or some interesting buttons on a string.

CREATIVE CURTAINS

Are you planning to sew your own curtains or work with your parents on this project? Then remember what you read about color and prints and think about the style of your room, too.

Many people use bed sheets to make curtains. This way you can easily have curtains that match your sheets. Two twin sheets can be made into curtains for a standard window by simply sewing a hem along the top to make an opening big enough for the size curtain rod you are using. If the sheets are too long, they can be hemmed, or "bunched up" above a ribbon or other kind of tieback.

You can also try this bunching-up trick on any plain straight curtains you have, if they are long enough. Puff them up into fluffy gathers above a tied ribbon or fabric loop tieback. This will give you a "balloon" effect.

Here's another trick with sheets: Hem an opening along the top that will fit on your curtain rod. Hang the sheets on the rod. Instead of using tiebacks, make a big, loose knot in each sheet about two-thirds of the way down from the rod. Fasten it to the wall with pins or tacks that won't show.

If you make curtains out of washable cotton fabrics, you can use fabric crayons or paint to add stripes, flowers and other designs. These paints include instructions, and you can find books full of design ideas. If you or a friend have artistic flair, this might be your choice.

Would you like to make some curtains without sewing hems? Buy felt from the fabric store. Cut it to fit your window, allowing two or three extra inches on top to sew the opening that will be gathered across the rod. Deena made a set of dark-blue felt curtains, then sewed cutouts on them in a "nighttime sky" design: a crescent moon, stars, Saturn and so on. Ver-ry interesting!

By now, you must agree that walls, floors *and* windows can be decorated in all kinds of ways, regardless of your budget!

Beautiful Beds

You spend nearly one-third of your life in your bed, so it's a really important place. There's nothing like a good night's sleep to pep you up for the next day; and what feels better than curling up under a cozy pile of quilts or blankets on a cold winter night? Your bed is certainly a major piece of furniture in your room. Even if your family just moved to a new house or apartment and you must wait to buy other furniture, you need some kind of place to sleep.

So, first of all, you want your bed to be comfortable. You're going to sleep there, but it's also a place to enjoy "alone time": to read or think quietly, to make plans for the next day or to dream about the future.

There are several different kinds of beds, but most of us have standard twin or double size mattresses and frames. Some girls have bunk beds, which helps to save floor space. If you are shopping for a new bed, you'll have to decide whether to get a headboard. If you want a headboard, you can choose from metals like steel and brass, various wood tones or painted woods, or maybe wicker or straw.

HINTS FOR HEADBOARDS

Does you headboard need a lift? If it's wood or wicker, a fresh coat of paint might be all it needs. You can also dress up plain painted headboards with paint, stencils, stick-on designs or decals. Jerri perked up her headboard by attaching a design of birds across the front. Ellen bordered hers in hearts and flowers. Trudy covered her worn-out wooden headboard with a large, thin fan that she found at a flea market.

You can also cover your headboard with fabric. Attach the fabric to the back of a wooden headboard with a staple gun. Or attach the fabric along the front outer edges of the headboard with upholstery tacks. Some girls cover their headboards with sheets that match their beds.

If you don't have a headboard, you could paint one on the wall behind your bed. Simply outline a "headboard" with masking tape and paint inside the outline. (Try painting a rectangle in one color, then using masking tape to paint a two- or three-inch border in another color.) If you and your roommate have twin beds, you could paint the "headboards" and their borders in the opposite color combinations; for example, you would have a green headboard with a blue border and she would have a blue headboard with a green border.

IMAGINATIVE HEADBOARDS

✪ Use a wallpaper border (maybe a geometric design?) for a "pasted-on" headboard.

✪ Paste panels of wallpaper—enough to match the width of your bed—just behind the bed from floor to ceiling.

✪ Get a ruffled curtain valance and attach it over your bed. You can buy decorative tacks in attractive shapes, like flowers, to stick the ruffles to the wall, if your parents agree.

IS IT A BED . . . OR A SOFA?

Would you like your bed to look less like a bed and more like a sofa? This is a good way to make your room serve a dual purpose—a bedroom at night, but a living room or a study during the day. A twin or double bed without a headboard can give you this look. (Note: If your bed frame has a headboard, you could remove the headboard or choose not to use the bed frame at all. Just put your mattress and box spring directly on the floor or leave them on the frame.)

This is one way to get a "sofa" look:

★★★

Creating a Sofa Bed

1. Put the bed's long side against the wall (in the center of the wall, if there's enough room). If you are using a frame, go directly to step 8.
2. If you are *not* using a bed frame, you can cover your box spring with a coordinating sheet. First, put a flat twin or double-size sheet *right side down* on the floor.
3. Put the box spring *right side down* in the middle of the sheet.
4. Start on any side of the box spring. Stretch the sheet over it; staple it all around, placing staples about three inches apart.
5. At each of the four corners, gather the fabric into neat, even pleats.
6. Now you can turn the box spring over and put it in place against the wall.
7. Lay the mattress on top and put on its coordinating sheet. (Go to step 9.)
8. Use a bedcover that looks "sofa-like"—plain corduroy or velveteen, for example—in a tailored style that falls to the floor.
9. Place two large pillows or a row of pillows against the back wall.
10. Add some smaller pillows in different shapes and sizes for an excellent finish!

★★★

If there is room at either end of your "sofa bed," you could put a trunk or a lamp table there. Decorate the wall above with posters or other wall hangings. You could also lay a "throw" (small blanket) on the bed—a fake fur or an afghan, for example.

BEDCOVERS FOR SWEET DREAMS

If you've shopped for sheets lately, you know that bed linens have come a long way since the homespun cloth of pioneer days and the white sheets of our grandmothers! There are plain sheets in an array of pastels and brights, stripes and geometric patterns galore, florals in light, bright or dark color combinations, even sets of coordinated sheets—different patterns that go together.

Whatever your style or color choice, you should be able to find sheets that you like. And don't forget the different tricks you've learned for decorating things made of fabric. Sheets, bedspreads and pillowcases can all be trimmed with ruffles, lace and ribbons. If you know how to embroider, you can add a personal touch to your bedspread, quilt or comforter by sewing your initials onto the middle or on one of the corners.

If you have a quilt that's faded or is the wrong color for you but is basically still in good shape, consider buying a quilt cover. You can buy them (in white, plain colors or prints) to fit different-sized comforters. These covers cost less than a new comforter.

Revitalize Your Bedspread

1. Starting at the hem of one of the corners at the bottom of your bedspread, sew straight up about four inches. Pull the loose end of the thread to make gathers and tie a knot to hold the gathers together. Attach a tassel or bow. Do the same for the other bottom corner of your bedspread.
2. Make the same kind of gathers all along the sides and bottom of the spread, about twelve inches apart, and finish them with your choice of trim, as above. Add a dust ruffle if the bed frame shows.
3. Paint a center design (maybe a rainbow, a bouquet, or an animal) with fabric paint or crayons.

★★★

PILES OF PILLOWS!

Along with the bed pillow you use each night, you can also put decorative pillows on your bed and in other parts of your room. Pillows are a great way to add color, texture and pattern to a room. By covering old pillows or plain foam pillow forms, you can have pillows without spending a fortune.

To stimulate your creativity, picture pillows used in these ways: a bedspread in a white, pink, turquoise and banana yellow floral print covered with small pillows in solid fabrics the same colors as those in the print; a red, white, and black striped spread on the bed with pillows in shiny polka-dotted fabrics in combinations of red and white, black and white, and black and red; a white eyelet bedspread with pillows in pastel lace with ribbon trim; a navy blue corduroy bedspread with pillows in emerald green and white; a petal-pink bedspread covered with pillows in different shades of pink—light, medium, dark.

✫✫ QUICK PILLOW QUIZ ✫✫

Now try to match these pillows:
1. *A pair of gold corduroy pillows*
2. *Floor pillows in black and white swirl designs*
3. *Pink satin pillows with lace*
4. *Purple and green plaid taffeta pillows*

With a room that has:
- a. An off-white bed frame; pale blue and white striped curtains and a pink, white and pale blue plaid bedspread
- b. Glossy lilac walls, gray carpet, a purple bedspread and a green lounge chair
- c. A four-poster cherry wood bed; red, gold and blue striped curtains; a brass lamp and two small chairs
- d. A red carpet, white walls, old records framed and hung on walls, and white wooden window shutters with black knobs.

Check your answers: 1. c; 2. d; 3. a; 4. b. Did you guess all four? By now, you are getting to be a decorating whiz! Try to figure out why all of the other things were chosen to go in each room, too.

MAKING PILLOWS

Jumbo pillows are fun for floors. You can buy large-sized pillows in variety stores and re-cover them if the colors or prints don't go with your room. Old furniture cushions can become floor pillows, too. Maybe you know someone who plans to get rid of an old sofa or chair. See if one of the cushions is in good enough shape to use "as is" or to re-cover for a floor pillow.

You can also make a super-size (or regular-size) pillow by stuffing shredded foam or pillow filler material (from the fabric store) into a home-sewn fabric container. The amount of fabric you need to make the container depends, of course, on the size of the pillow you are making.

Pillow Making

For a large pillow three feet by four feet, you will need:

- ✪ About 3–4 yards of 45″ or 54″ wide muslin to make an inner pillow to hold the foam; the same amount of decorative fabric for the pillow cover.
- ✪ Foam filler material. Check the package to see how much of the filler is needed for the size pillow you are making—some filling materials are bulkier than others.

This is how to make it:
1. Make the muslin liner. Start by folding it in two and then cut along the fold. (This makes it

easier to stuff the pillow evenly.) Cut it to the right size, leaving an extra inch all around.

2. Sew the muslin together on three sides with the right sides of the fabric facing each other. Sew about ¾″ from the edge. Leave a 24″ opening on one side to insert the stuffing. Turn the sewn muslin holder right side out.

3. Fill the muslin liner evenly with the foam material. (Hint: Open the bag of foam and stick it inside the pillow container, then start pushing the foam inside—fewer spills!)

4. Stitch the open edges of the pillow together.

5. Now make the decorative pillow case. It should be slightly larger (about ½″ on each side) than the stuffed muslin case.

6. Stitch three sides together with the right sides of the fabric facing each other. Turn it right side out.

7. Put the foam-filled muslin into the fabric case. Now you can finish the pillow case by stitching the open edges together. Fold an even hem on each side and pin the folded edges together so they are hidden inside. Sew neat stitches across the top so that they don't show.

★★★

To cover foam pillow forms that you buy at the store, use steps 5–7 for making the outer case (the decorative fabric part) of the pillow. For a standard 14-inch-square pillow form, cut two pieces of fabric about 17 inches square. Check the fit before sewing the final edges shut.

"NO-SEW" PILLOWS

Do you have some tired-looking pillows or plain pillow forms you want to cover—without sewing a stitch? You can use a piece of fabric or a pretty bandanna or scarf to "wrap and tie" your pillows. You'll have pretty (maybe one-of-a-kind) pillows in minutes!

Using a square pillow form (14"-16") and a 32"-square scarf or piece of hemmed fabric, you can cover a pillow like this:

Knotty Pillows

1. Lay the pillow form on the middle of the fabric so that the fabric forms a diamond shape around the square of the pillow.
2. Bring one corner of fabric across the pillow. Bring the opposite corner over it, folding about four inches of the pointed corner underneath itself to make a neat, straight edge.
3. Bring the other two corners neatly together. Smooth their sides. Tie the two pointed ends into a knot at the center of the pillow. You can leave the ends of the knots hanging freely or tuck them under the folds of the fabric. Lay your pillow on a chair or bed with the plain side or the knotted side showing—whichever look you like best.

Turn a tired pillow into a terrific pillow to spice up your room.

Another way to wrap, using the same size pillow and scarf/fabric:

Candy Pillows

1. Place the pillow in the middle of the fabric so its corners point in the same direction as the corners of the fabric.
2. Fold the fabric over the pillow on two opposite sides.
3. Gather the fabric on each of the other two sides of the pillow and twist them like the ends of wrapped candy. Then use rubber bands to secure each one. Tie yarn or ribbon over the rubber band. (Hint: You can use two scarves in prints or colors that look good together and tie them in the way described above.)

With just a little sewing, you can use a 22″-square scarf (cotton bandanna, silk-like polyester, etc.) to cover a pillow form that is 14 to 16 inches square:

★★★

Neat Pillows

1. Lay the pillow form on the fabric on the diagonal—so the fabric forms a diamond shape around the square pillow.
2. Bring the edges up—two opposite ends at a time.
3. Stitch the last edges together as neatly and invisibly as you can.

How does your bed look now? Are you working on bedcovers or pillows, a behind-the-bed wall treatment—or are you already done? With a little thought, effort and imagination, your bed can be a pleasure to look at as well as to sleep in!

Special Touches Make a Difference!

*P*icture a room with four painted walls, curtains at the window and a bed. Now add a table desk with a lamp and chair, a small shelving unit and an overhead light. Who do you think lives there?

Probably nobody! The room above sounds like an empty room in a hotel or a dormitory. What's missing? Those dozens of small items that add personality—and sometimes clutter!—to a room.

Accessories say a lot about what kinds of activities and interests are important to the room's owner.

What accessories do you see in your own room? Some of them are probably just for decoration, such as paper flowers, artwork on the walls or china figurines. Others are really useful—pens and pencils, storage boxes, a dictionary. Often, accessories serve two purposes: They are useful *and* decorative. Examples of this are a crystal paperweight, a pretty desk blotter and a pair of hand-painted bookends.

Maybe some of the accessories you have now could be painted or otherwise decked out to make your room more attractive. Or maybe you need some new containers for things and would like to save money by making them yourself. Read on!

ALL KINDS OF CONTAINERS

Different small containers can hold everything that's lying around loose in your room, from pencils and paper clips to jewelry and scarves. Look around for glass, wood or china containers that nobody wants. Sometimes, you can get unusual ones for pennies at a yard sale. Start by collecting used jars, frozen-juice cans, milk cartons and cardboard boxes with an eye toward making them work well for you—all spruced up, of course!

Cleaned frozen-juice cans can be made into holders for pens and pencils. Spray-paint them or cover them with self-sticking paper. A set of small containers in the same print, or two that go together like florals and stripes, might be nice if the patterns go with your room.

You can use paint or self-sticking paper on coffee cans, too. Try adding some sticker trims to these new containers or stenciling them. A coat of polyurethane over the paint will "seal" it and keep it from chipping.

AMAZING ACCESSORIES

There are lots of accessories you can make yourself that will really liven up your room. Making a one-of-a-kind jewelry box is really easy and will look great and be useful too! Simply take an ordinary metal tool or tackle box and spray it with pastel, brightly colored, or gold or silver spray paint. Cut squares of pretty velveteen or other nice fabric to line the compartments inside. Maybe you'd like the outside to be really flashy? Attach stick-on jewels from a crafts store (or glue on beads or other glittery pieces from your own broken jewelry).

Clean jars or bottles can be filled with marbles and used as doorstops, bookends or holders for dried flowers on longish stems or branches. Nina made an interesting decoration by filling a long jar with marbles and arranging some white-painted tree branches in it.

Try making a map-covered file box—it's handy to have around and will look great:

World-Class Files

1. Measure each section of the box and allow at least an extra ¾" all around for folding over the edges.

2. Use a ruler and pencil to mark the cutting lines on the back of the map and then cut it out.
3. Use spray adhesive to glue it to the box.
4. Fold the edges around so they lie flat and the entire box is covered neatly.
5. To keep it clean, apply two coats of fixative spray from an art supply store or drugstore. (Note: You can also use wallpaper, gift wrap or certain kinds of fabric for this kind of box covering.)

Bricks can make interesting bookends or doorstops. Start by sealing the bricks with a few coats of sealer—the clay is very porous—then use acrylic or house paint to paint them the color of your choice. You can use stencils or paint a freehand design on the bricks. A layer of fixative spray on top protects the paint and design. These bricks could also be covered with fabric, attached by spray adhesive.

Round decorator tables can hold lamps and other accessories. These unfinished tables have three legs that you screw underneath the round base. They are fairly inexpensive and can be found in department or housewares stores. You can cover them with round cloths that are sold in the stores, then add a square cloth on top in a pattern and color that you like. Either use a scarf or hem a square of fabric for this cloth covering.

Collect attractive pieces of fabric for these kinds of decorating projects. They can be used as dresser scarves, too. So can an old piece of cleaned-up lace from an attic. You can make your own dresser scarf by sewing together a few rows of pretty white five-and-dime store handkerchiefs. The number of hankies you need depends on the amount of dresser-top you want to cover and also the size of the hankies. Lay them out so they form a square or rectangle and sew the adjoining edges together as neatly as possible. They do not need a hem and are already pretty because of their design.

Have you seen round straw placemats in the stores? They come in pretty colors and can be made into "wall flowers." Try hanging them in a corner, one on each wall. Cut green leaves and stems from self-sticking paper and press them on under the flowers. Add a straw wastebasket or clothes hamper to look like a flower pot!

There are many things you can do to liven up mirrors. If you have a plain unframed mirror on your wall, you could fasten lengths of ribbon at each side (use tacks to do this). Now attach mementoes like postcards, photos or notes on the ribbons. (You can pin them or use double-faced tape.)

Another frame for a plain mirror can be made from a length of fishnet draped over the top and sides. You can lay things inside the netting, if the objects are not too heavy. Items that might fall out can be fastened on with wire or pretty ribbons.

QUICK ACCESSORY PROJECTS

- ✪ Large *seashells* from a beach trip or a store can hold many small things.

103

- If you have a plain *tissue holder* from the five-and-dime store, you can cover it using wallpaper or gift wrap.
- A basket with a cover can be flat enough to serve as a *small table* for a lamp, books, etc. Put a scarf or bandanna across the top.
- A piece of plywood painted like the walls can be put on top of a radiator as a *shelf* to hold small photographs, a vase of leaves, etc.
- An inexpensive *paper lantern* can be hung below your lighting fixture. Make sure the paper is thin enough to let plenty of light pass through.
- If you have a glass top on your *dresser*, you can make it extra pretty by putting a piece of pretty fabric or wallpaper, cut to fit, under the glass.

GROWING THINGS

You'll probably want at least one plant in your room. You can put them in decorative containers or use clay pots. These pots are nice whether they are painted to match your room or left natural. Use a sealer before applying paint.

A row of inexpensive red or white geraniums in pots on the windowsill is a nice look for many rooms. You can find other inexpensive plants that are not difficult to care for. Be sure to find out how much (direct or indirect) sunlight your plant will need and how often it should be watered.

Plants add pizzazz to any room as long as they are properly cared for.

105

You can bring living beauty into your room in other ways, as well. Try floating some pretty leaves or seasonal blossoms in a bowl of water. You can also arrange such things as leaves, Queen Anne's lace or pussy willows in containers. And don't forget branches—either left natural or painted.

A NICE-SMELLING RETREAT

Your room will give you extra pleasure if it not only looks good, but *smells* nice, too. Why not make some sachets to hang in closets and tuck in drawers—under your pillow, too. You can buy potpourri by the bagful in drugstores and variety stores, as well as gift shops. There are all kinds of delicious scents to choose from: fruit smells like lemon and peach, ginger or mixtures of spices, single florals or mixed bouquets. You will also need some pretty fabric, a pair of scissors and some yarn to tie the bags. This is how Christine made sachets for her room:

Stunning Sachets

1. Cut squares of the fabric 6″ x 6″. Use pinking shears, if you have them, for a prettier edge.
2. Place a tablespoonful of potpourri in the middle of the square.
3. Gather the edges of the cloth square into the middle to make a bundle. Tie a 12″ long ribbon or piece of yarn around the "neck" of the sachet bag.

With ideas like these and many of your own, your room will steadily develop its own personality. It certainly will *not* look like the empty, un-lived-in space described at the beginning of this chapter—not when you give it so much loving care!

Putting It All Together

*A*fter reading this far, you know that there's a lot to think about when you decorate a room. Fixing up a whole room from start to finish means making decisions about floor plans, colors, accessories, patterns and prints, storage areas and activity spaces and a whole lot more! But along with the work comes the fun of making a room that fits your needs and suits your personality and tastes. And when someone admires something in your room there's also the fun of saying: "I made that!"

You've read some of the different ways that other girls have decorated their rooms. Maybe some of these same ideas would be just right for *your* room—or will give you a good idea of your own.

ROOMS WITH A "THEME"

If you're still unsure about what special overall look you want in your room, you might like to consider decorating around a special "theme." Many people find that this way of decorating comes to them naturally, because they have a strong interest or a hobby that takes over when they're doing the room. Other people work on a particular theme because they like to see their interests expressed throughout the room. Theme decorating can be a pleasure—and there are many kinds to choose from.

Suppose, for example, that you're a music lover, like Marianne. How can you express this in your space and surround yourself with musical things? You might start by using record album covers and musician posters to decorate your walls. Marianne put a few "gold records" (old records sprayed gold) over her bed and made a big felt G clef to decorate her bulletin board. You could also choose to frame old sheet music, have musical notes on your bedspread or display one or more instruments on a shelf. This will make a room really *sing*.

Heather chose a seashore theme for her room. Her walls are painted a light sea-blue, and the five small pillows on her bed are covered in fabrics that contain

110

different seashell patterns. She found a fabulous way to display her shell collection: She put them inside a long piece of fishnet that hangs across the whole wall behind her bed. There is even a propped-up beach umbrella over the side of her desk.

Would you like to live in a garden? A "garden theme" room might include a grassy green carpet, sky-blue walls and lots of floral prints in the bedspread, curtains, sheets and pillows. Pretty homemade cloth or paper flowers and a plant or two add more to the "garden."

Eve's favorite things are books and in decorating her room, she has made use of them in all sorts of creative ways. She found sketches of some of her favorite writers and made "silhouette" pictures of them by cutting the outlines of their heads in black paper. Each cutout was then mounted on plain white paper and the author's name was inscribed on the bottom. Eve also hung some of her favorite book jackets on the walls between the silhouettes. For her birthday, someone gave her a bookstand frame to hold her favorite book open on her desk. Her desk also has a pretty juice-jar container to hold bookmarks Eve has made from different colored ribbons.

You can see how a special interest leads to more and more special touches for your room. Plus you have the pleasure of being surrounded by the things you love! Having a theme room also gives you a goal for some of your shopping trips. It helps you to keep your mind on a total effect. The resulting room looks "pulled together." Another nice thing about having a special interest or collection is that people remember what you like. Often, they will know the perfect gift to give you—something that fits with the theme of your room!

WHEN THERE'S A PROBLEM . . .

As you've read the previous chapters, you've learned many ways to solve the problems that come with decorating a room. You've discovered ways to live more happily with a roommate, how to beat the "battle of the budget" and how to make the most of what you have. It's sometimes helpful to remember that these problems are common. Think of Terry, for example. Terry was miserable when she saw her new room in the house her family had just bought. The room had previously belonged to a seventeen-year-old boy. It had a soiled red shag carpet (which Terry had to live with) and off-white (very dingy) paint on three walls. The fourth wall was covered with cork tiles.

Now, Terry loves frilly, feminine things, so how could she ever make over this room into *her* style? It took some looking around, some sewing and some patience, but over the next year, Terry made her room really nice. Frilly white curtains with a pattern of small red dots helped. So did a white eyelet comforter and the pillows Terry covered with red and white floral and heart prints. Terry's parents said she could choose a new color for the walls, so she picked a fresh, clean white. Right after that, Terry found a small, white, fluffy rug at a yard sale. After a thorough washing, it looked good on her floor and toned down the red carpet. As for the cork wall, Terry covered it with fabric in white, pink, and red stripes. She uses it as a bulletin board.

As with the other successful room "makeovers" described in this book, Terry learned to work with what she had. She communicated with her parents and worked out a plan for replacing or improving the things she wanted to change, as soon as the family budget permitted. In time, the room had Terry's personal touch and contained the pretty, girlish things she enjoys having around her.

These guidelines are pretty much the same ones that work in solving other kinds of problems: think, communicate and work in steps toward a solution. It pays off when you have a prettier, more comfortable room.

ENJOY YOUR ROOM!

No matter what stage of decorating your room is in—whether you are just beginning to fix it up or are putting on some final touches—the most important thing to remember is that this is *your* space and whatever you do to it should give you joy.

If you've been following a plan and using the ideas in this book, along with your own creativity, you can have a room that "works" and that is really *you*. Your decorated-by-you room will be ready when you need to finish your homework, sew on a button, hang around with friends or just sit by yourself. The closet and drawers will be arranged so that dressing is a pleasure. And there will be plenty of interesting wall decorations and other accessories to make you feel like you're surrounded by friends.

And, of course, a cozy bed to welcome you when you're ready to call it a day.

Maybe this is the first time you ever really decorated your room yourself. If it is, then it's just the beginning. There will be many more rooms to decorate in the future and each one will be better and better! So now it's time to take a look around and pat yourself on the back. You've done a super job—enjoy your room!

SMART TALK Has It All!

Some of the best tips for fashion, fun and friendship are in the Smart Talk series. Learn how to look and feel your greatest, create your own personal style, and show the world the great new you! Smart Talk points the way:

Skin Deep
Looking Good
Eating Pretty
Feeling Fit
Finishing Touches—Manners with Style
Now You're Talking—Winning with Words
Dream Rooms—Decorating with Flair
Great Parties—How to Plan Them
How to Make (and Keep) Friends